Molly the Mole

First published in 2018
by Jessica Kingsley Publishers
73 Collier Street
London N1 9BE, UK
and
400 Market Street, Suite 400
Philadelphia, PA 19106, USA

www.jkp.com

Library of Congress Cataloging in Publication Data
A CIP catalog record for this book is available from the Library of Congress

British Library Cataloguing in Publication Data
A CIP catalogue record for this book is available from the British Library

ISBN 978 1 78592 452 1
eISBN 978 1 78450 827 2

Printed and bound in China

Molly the Mole

A Story to Help Children Build Self-Esteem

ALICE REEVES

Illustrated by
PHOEBE KIRK

Part of the *Truth & Tails* series

Jessica Kingsley Publishers
London and Philadelphia

Molly the Mole had lots of friends,
because she enjoyed helping other
animals more than anything in the world.

When Daisy the Deer got her hoof stuck in a tangle of tree roots, Molly burrowed deep down into the ground to get her free.

When Belinda the Butterfly wanted to pick flowers from the meadow, Molly helped her to make a beautiful bouquet.

When Owen the Owl needed
help studying for a spelling test,
Molly tested him until he got
every single question right.

Even though
helping her
friends made
Molly very happy,
sometimes she
felt very different
from them.

She didn't know why, but
this made her feel sad.

The next time Molly went for a walk in the woods with Daisy the Deer, Daisy noticed that Molly wasn't having much fun.

"What's the matter, Molly?" asked Daisy.

"You love going for walks, but you don't look very happy today," she said.

"I feel sad because I don't have lovely long legs like you," sighed Molly.

"That's no reason to feel sad," said Daisy. "That's because you're not a deer! We need long legs for running through the woods."

Later that day, Molly the Mole
went to Belinda the Butterfly's
tree house for afternoon tea.

The flowers from the meadow were bright
and colourful, but Molly felt gloomy.

"What's bothering you, Molly?"
asked Belinda. "You don't seem
to be enjoying your tea."

"My tea is lovely!" said Molly.
"I'm feeling sad because my fur isn't
pretty colours like your wings."

"You don't need to feel sad about
that," said Belinda. "It's because you're
not a butterfly! We need colourful
wings to blend in with the flowers."

When she had finished her tea, Molly went to find out if Owen had passed his spelling test.

"I got an A-plus — that's the best mark you can get!" exclaimed Owen. "Let's celebrate!"

"I'm proud of you, Owen," said Molly, "but I'm not in the mood for a party."

"What's wrong, Molly?" asked Owen. "You love parties!"

"I know," said Molly. "I'm just sad because I'm not as clever as you. I could never get an A-plus in a spelling test."

"Please don't be sad Molly," said Owen. "That's because you're not an owl. Owls are very clever animals."

When Molly the Mole went back to her mole hill, she was still feeling sad.

She made her favourite food, a big juicy worm sandwich, to make herself feel better.

While she was eating her worm sandwich, there was a knock on her door.

It was Daisy, Belinda, and Owen!

"What are you all doing here?" asked Molly, popping her head out of her mole hill.

"We all noticed you were feeling sad today," said Daisy.

"We wanted to come and cheer you up," said Belinda.

"We wanted to tell you why
we love you," said Owen.

"Remember when I got my hoof caught in
the tree roots and you used your strong
arms to get me out?" asked Daisy.

"That was such a kind thing to do. I
wish everybody was as kind as you."

Daisy's words made Molly smile,
and she felt less sad.

"When I wanted to make my house
more cheerful, you made me a beautiful
bouquet of flowers," said Belinda.

"I couldn't have done that, because
I don't have claws. I wish everybody
could be as helpful as you."

Belinda's words made
Molly feel happier.

"I wouldn't have got an A-plus in my spelling test if you hadn't spent all that time helping me study," said Owen.

"You didn't even get annoyed when I got things wrong! I wish everybody could be as patient as you."

Owen's words made Molly's heart fill with happiness.

It was then that Molly realised she didn't love her friends because they were tall, or pretty, or clever.

She loved them for lots of different reasons.

She loved going for long, sunny
walks through the woodland
with Daisy the Deer.

She loved drinking tea and
eating cake with Belinda the
Butterfly in her tree house.

She loved listening to Owen the Owl talk about all the interesting things he knew.

Molly finally understood.

It doesn't matter what you look like or what special talents you have, as long as you are kind, helpful, and patient.

That's what makes people love you.

Just like
everybody
loves Molly.

Notes for Teachers and Parents

The following open questions can be asked to inspire discussion.

Circle time before reading

★ What is special about you? Think about something
    that may be different from other people.

★ Have you ever wished you had something someone else had?

★ Talk about the word "compare" and what it means.

★ Have you ever compared yourself to someone else?

After reading

★ Why does Molly feel sad?

★ What do her friends say that helps her feel better?

★ What does Molly realise is the most important thing about friends?

★ Tell the person next to you something you think is really special about them.

★ Why should we not compare ourselves to other people?

★ What do Molly and her friends teach us?

Resources

Childline has a number of resources for children around dealing with different feelings and emotions, including building confidence and self-esteem: https://www.childline.org.uk/info-advice/your-feelings/feelings-emotions

YoungMinds is the UK's leading charity championing the wellbeing and mental health of young people: http://youngminds.org.uk

Acknowledgements

Thank you to everyone who has supported the *Truth & Tails* series from the beginning – without your help these books wouldn't have been possible.

Also in the *Truth & Tails* series

Carlos the Chameleon
A Story to Help Empower Children to Be Themselves

As a chameleon, it's in Carlos's nature to change his colours in order to fit into his surroundings. Carlos is usually green, but can turn pink to join the flamingos, blue to match the frogs, and spotty to resemble the jaguars.

When the other animals find out that Carlos has been changing his colours in order to fit in, they reassure him that his own colour is beautiful and that he doesn't need to change who he is to be accepted and loved by his friends.

Roxy the Raccoon

A Story to Help Children Learn about Disability and Inclusion

Roxy lives in the forest with her three best friends, who she loves to visit and play games with. Roxy is in a wheelchair, so sometimes it is harder for her to go to the same places and play the same games as the other animals.

Roxy and her friends realise that by making a few small changes and working together, they can make the forest a better place for everyone. Roxy teaches us that there are plenty of ways to be more inclusive of those who have a disability so that everyone can join in.

Vincent the Vixen

A Story to Help Children Learn about Gender Identity

Vincent is a boy fox who loves to play dress up with their brothers and sisters, but when they always choose to dress up as female characters, Vincent's siblings begin to wonder why.

Vincent comes to realise that they are actually a girl fox, and with the support of friends and family they transition to living as their true self. This is the story of one fox's journey to realising their gender identity and the importance of being who you are.